# I LOVE FLOWERS

## A Coloring book

## T Renarda Rudolph

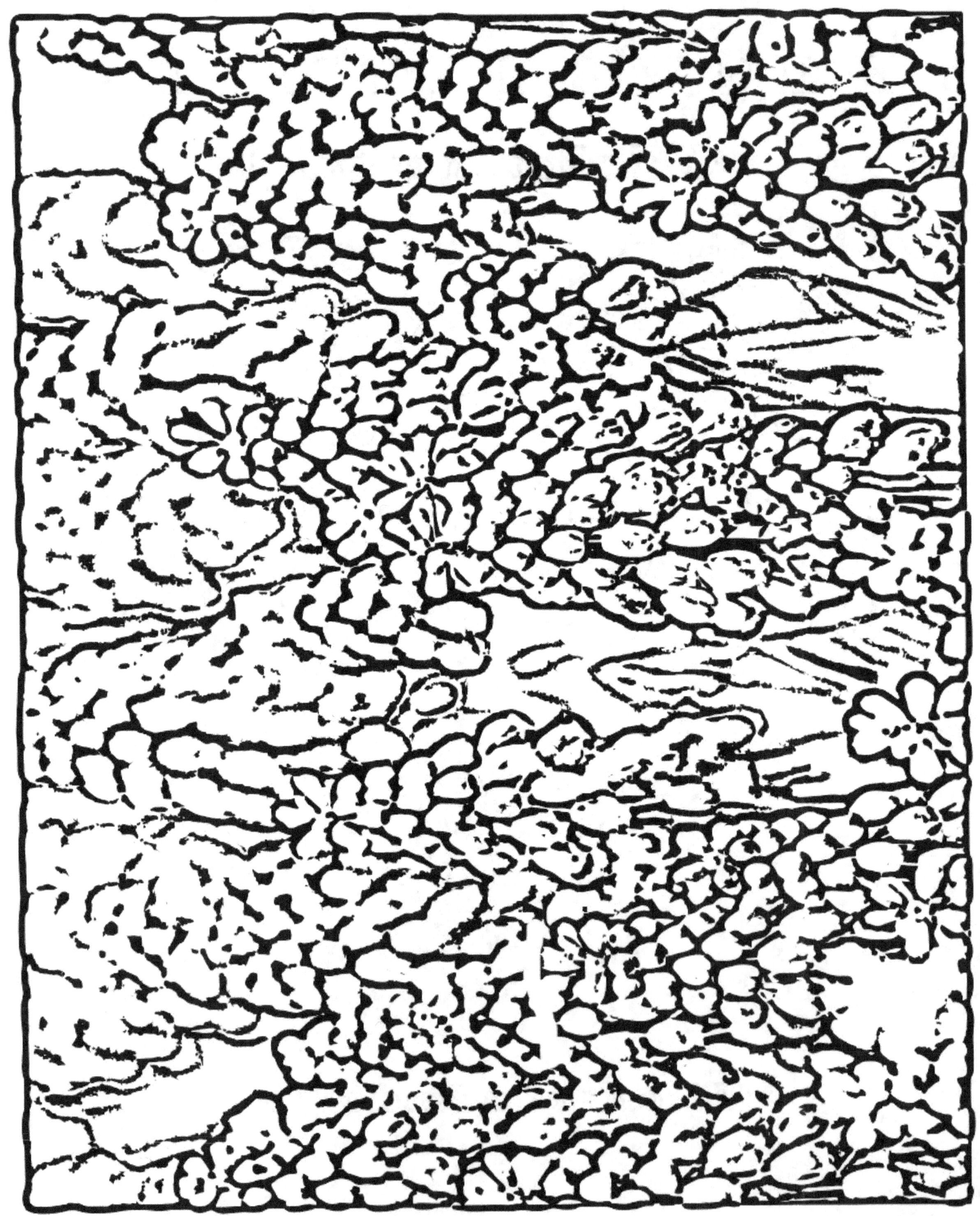

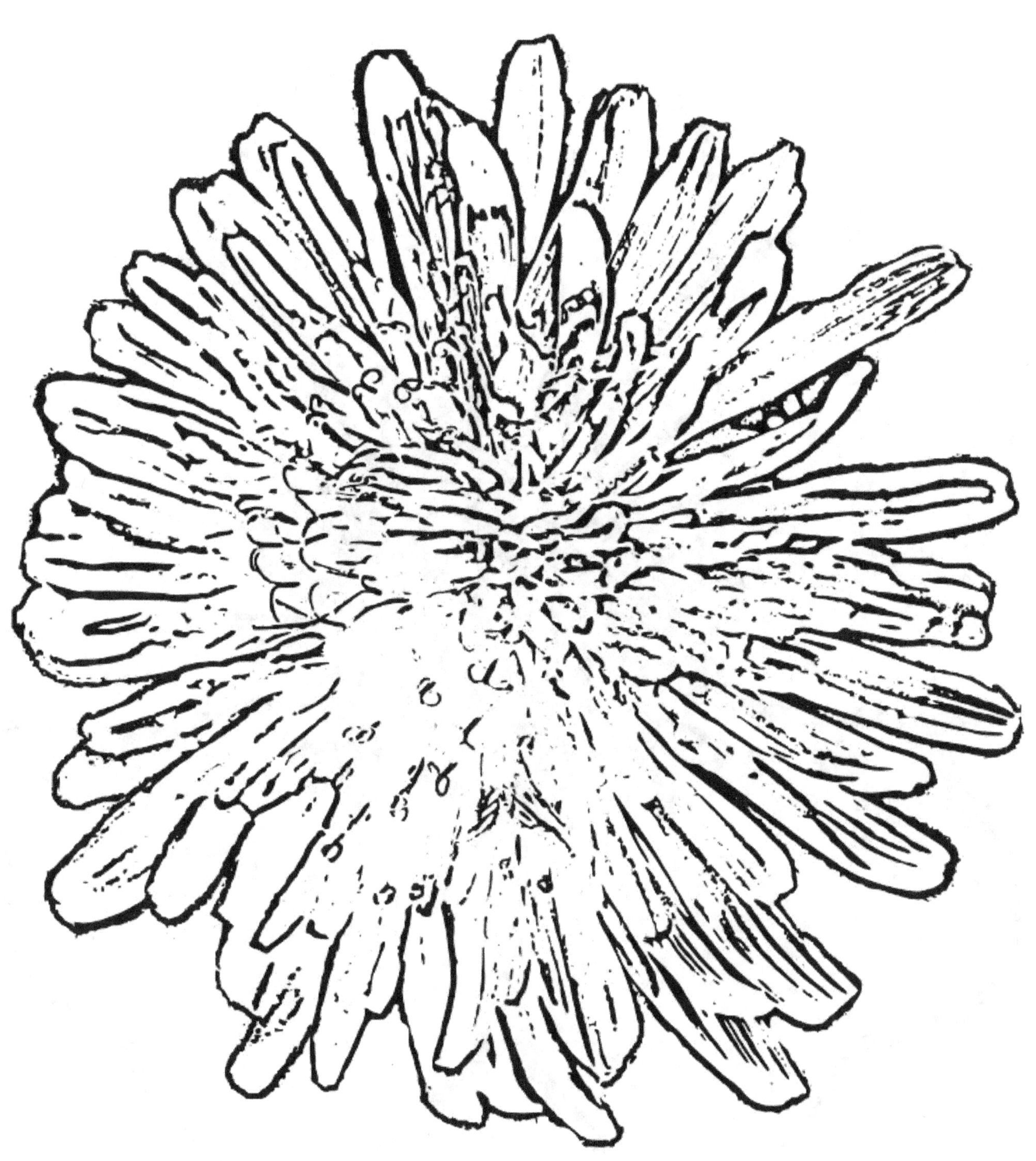

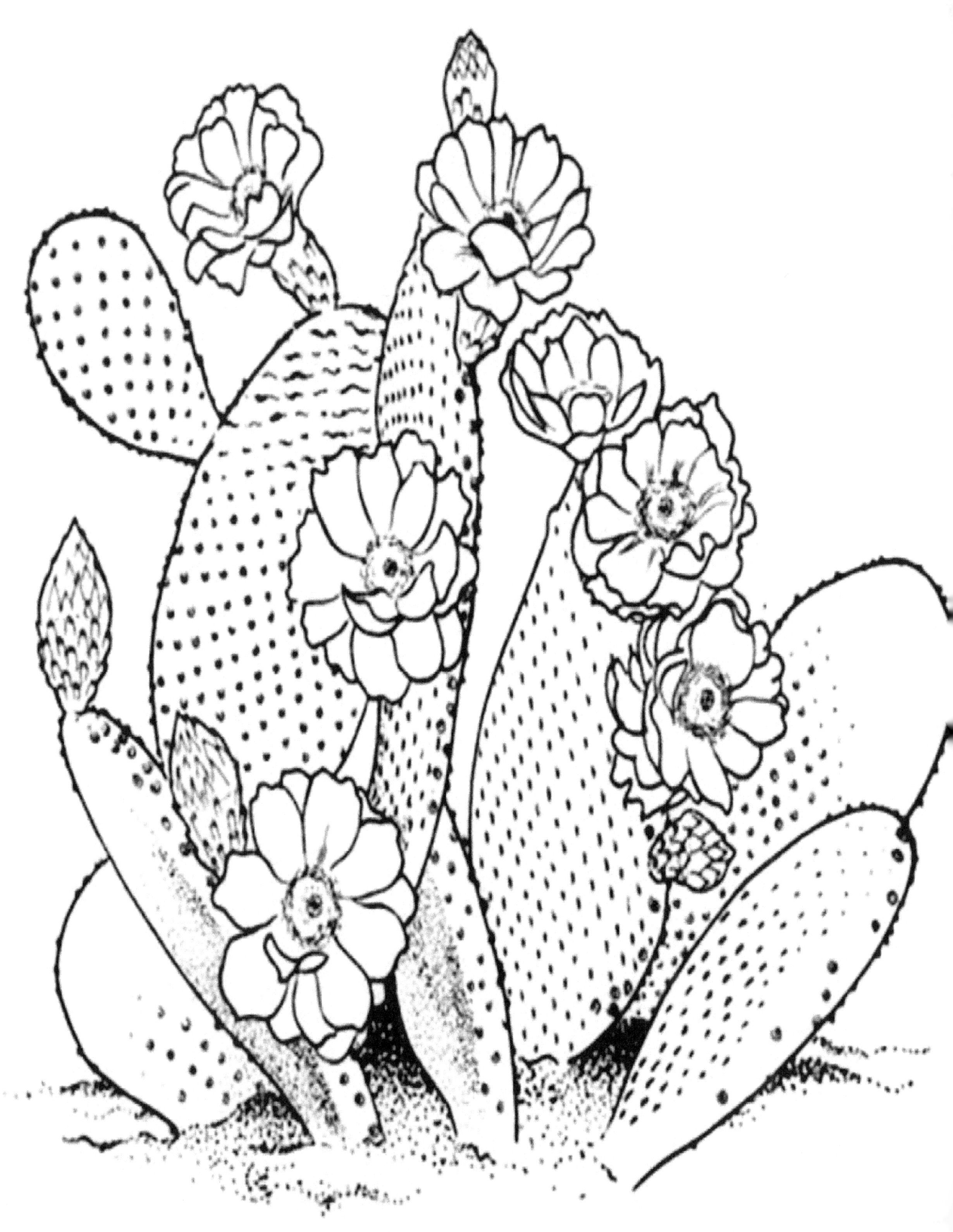

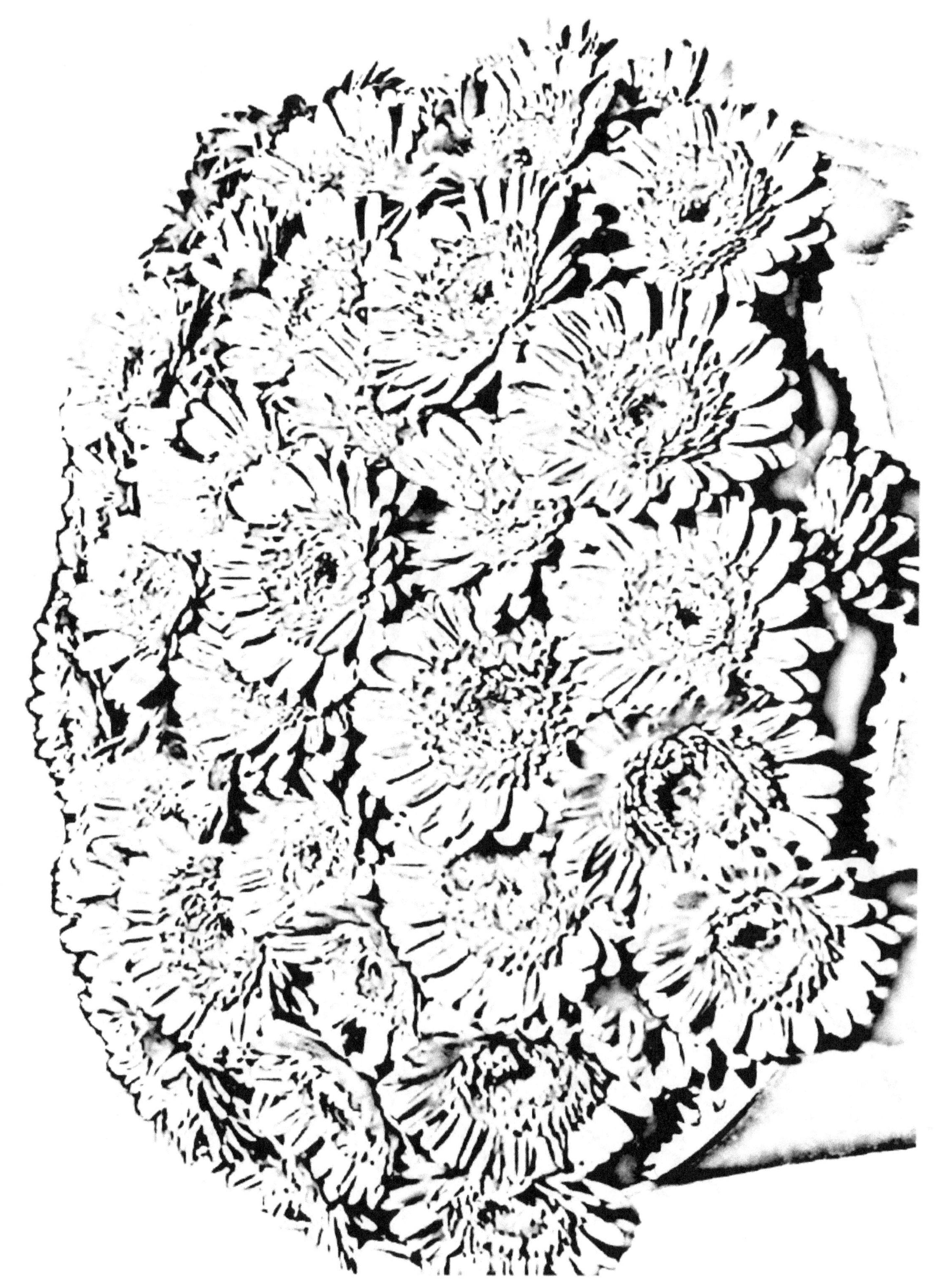

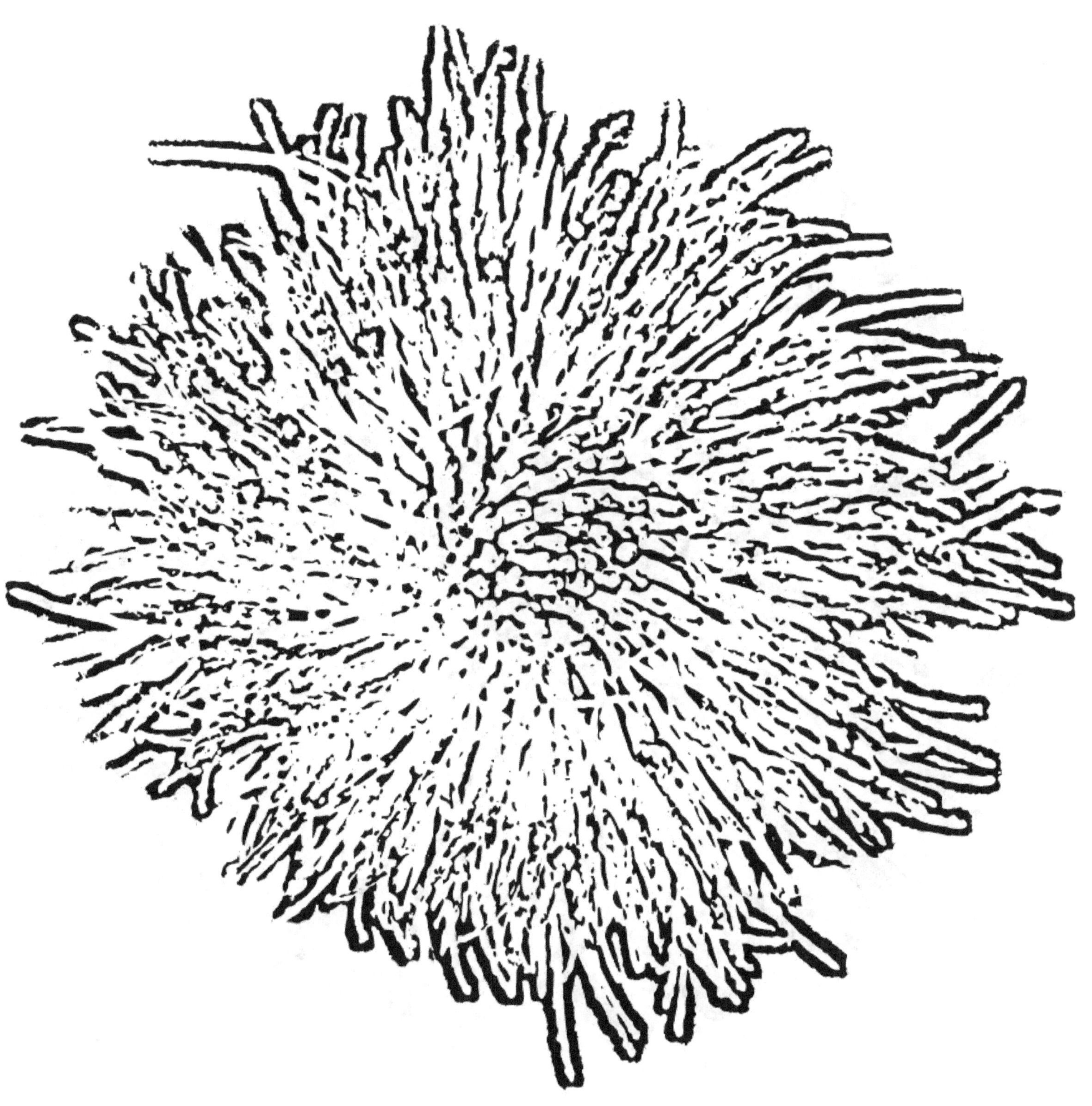

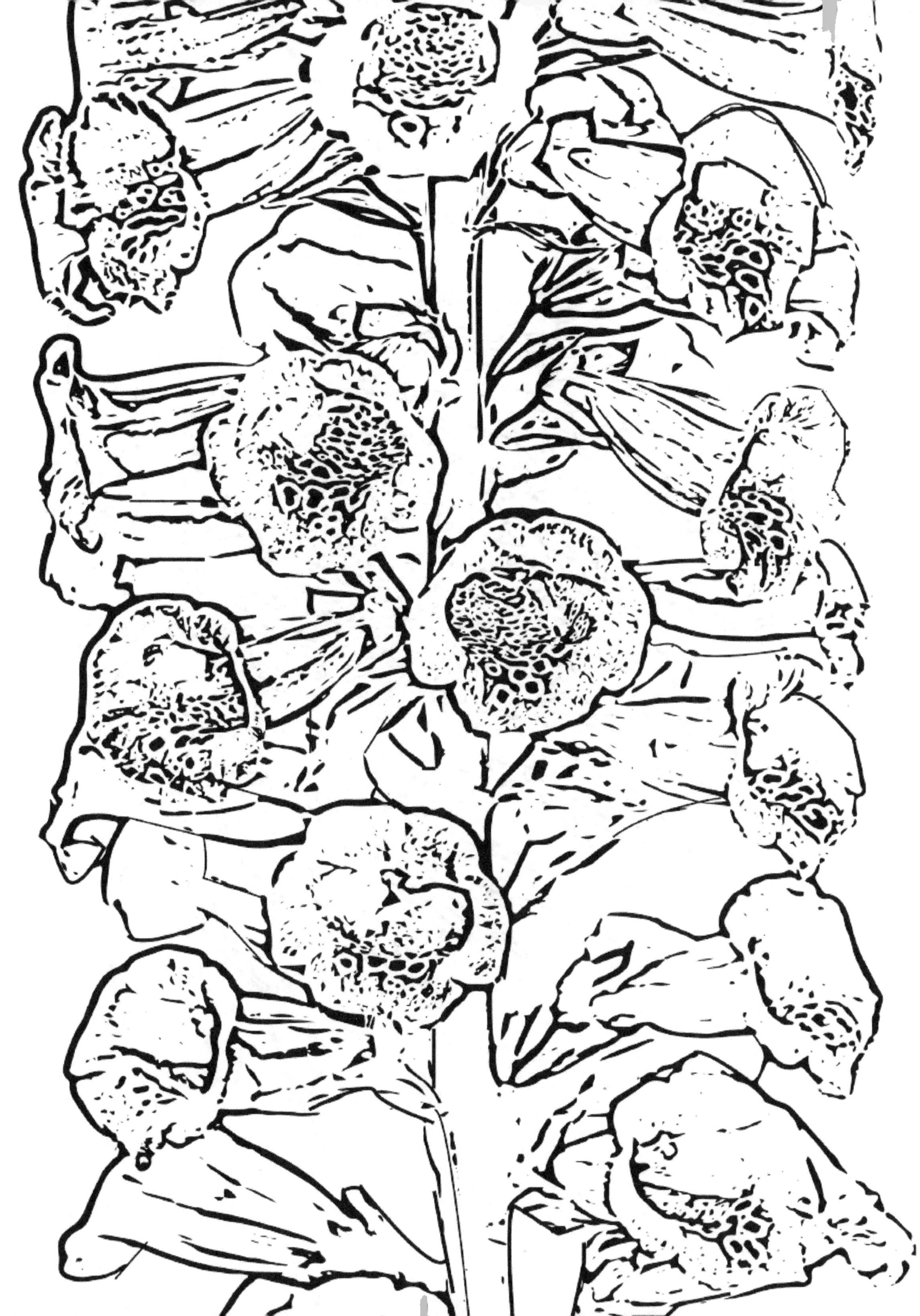

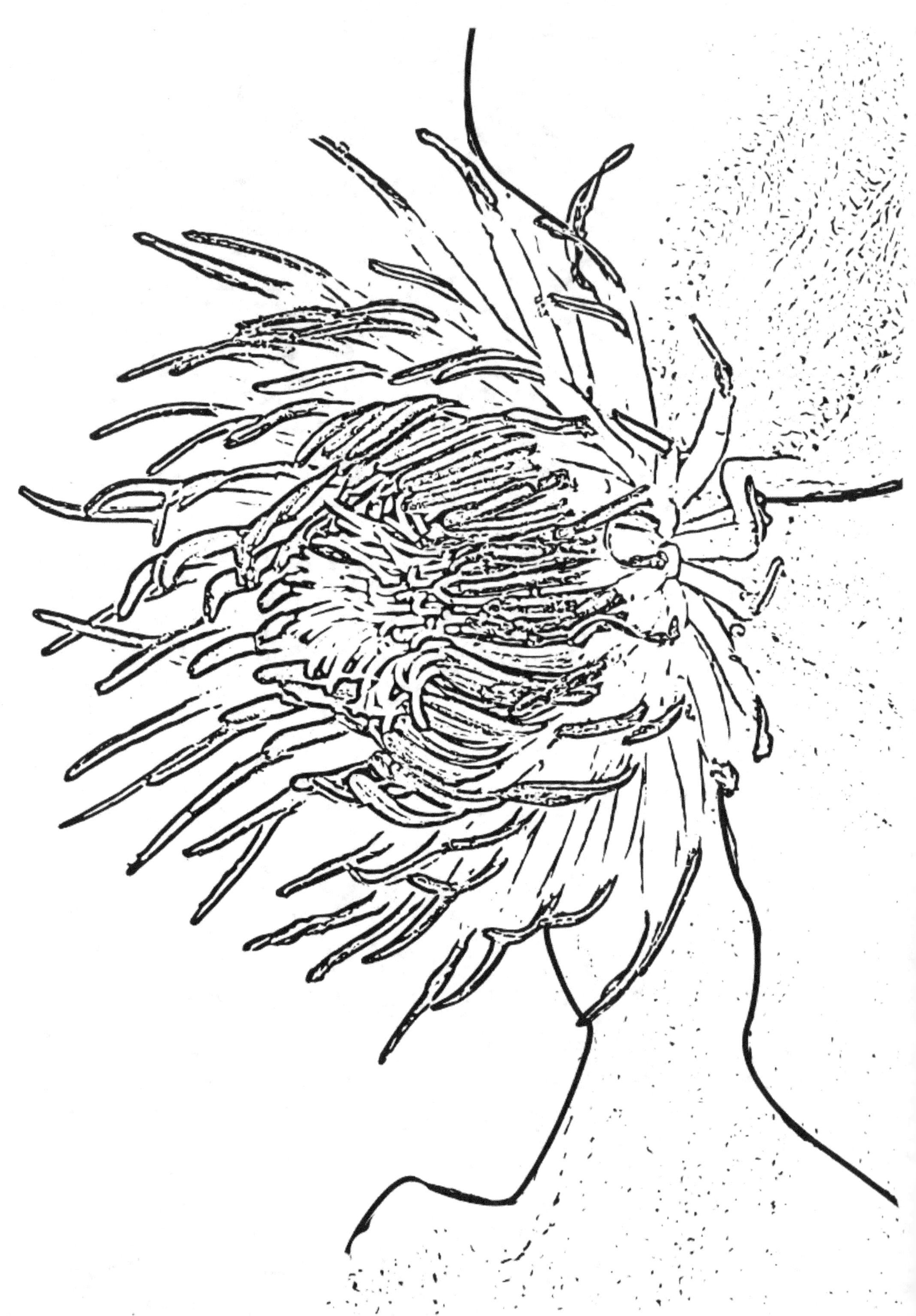

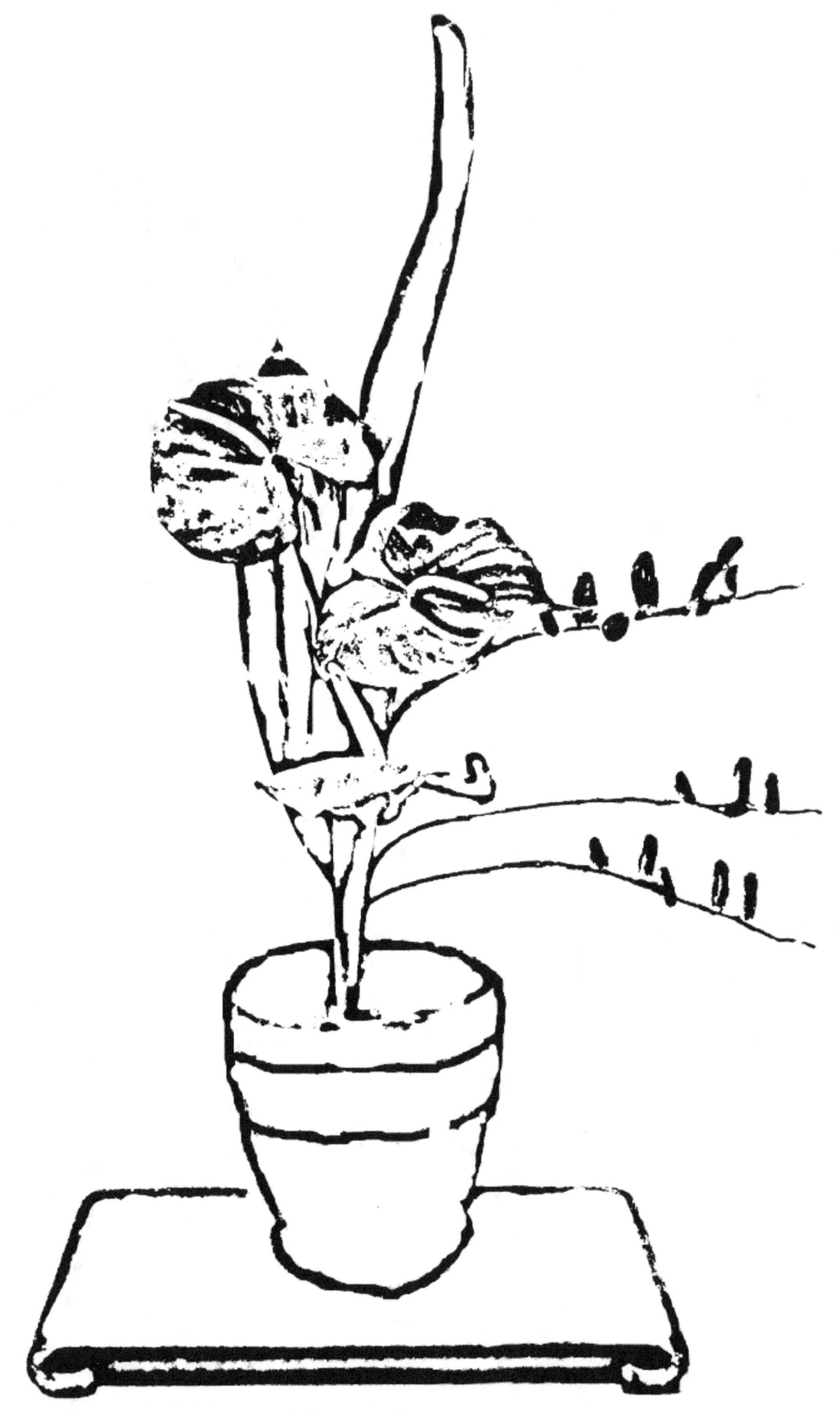

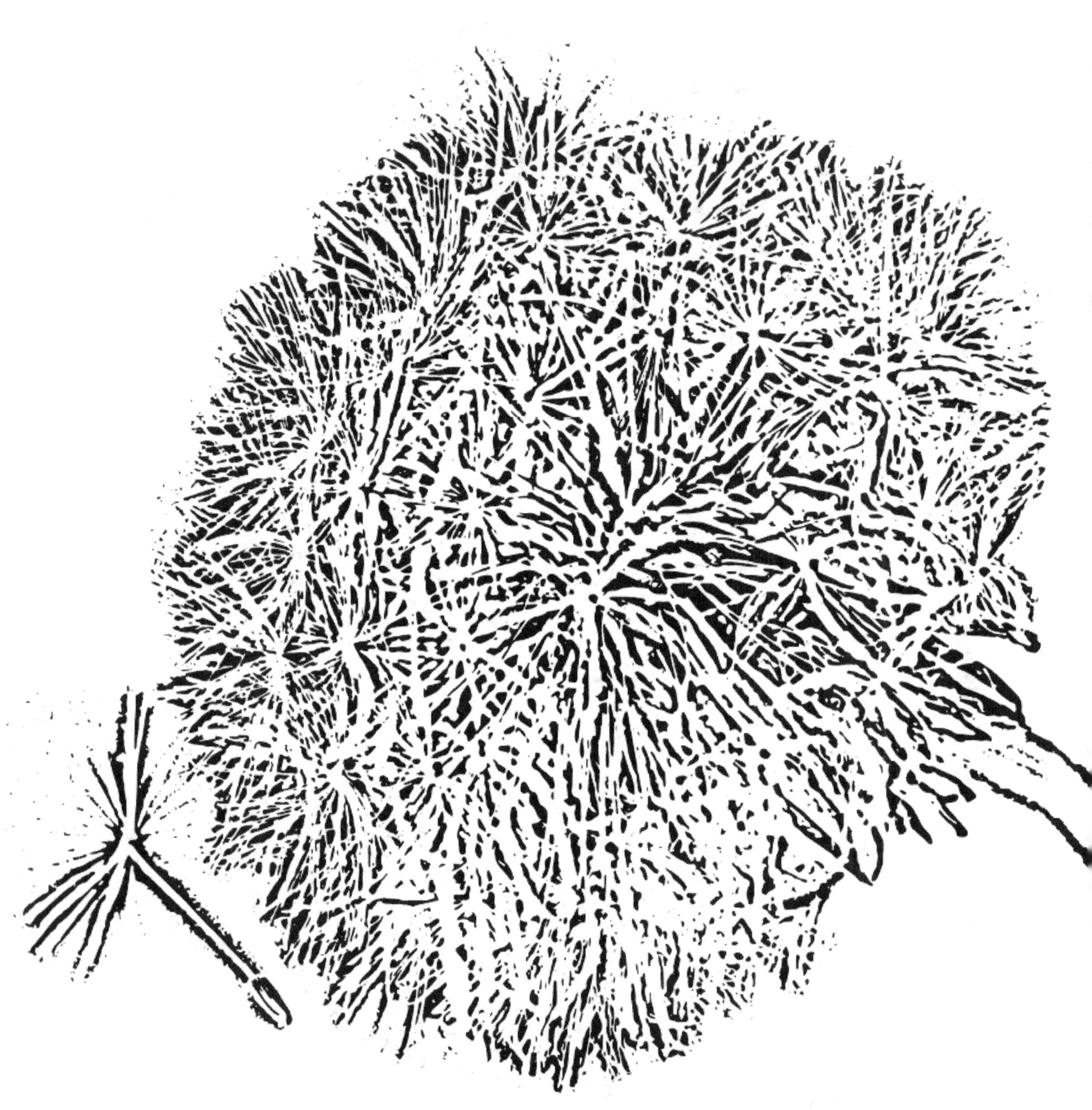

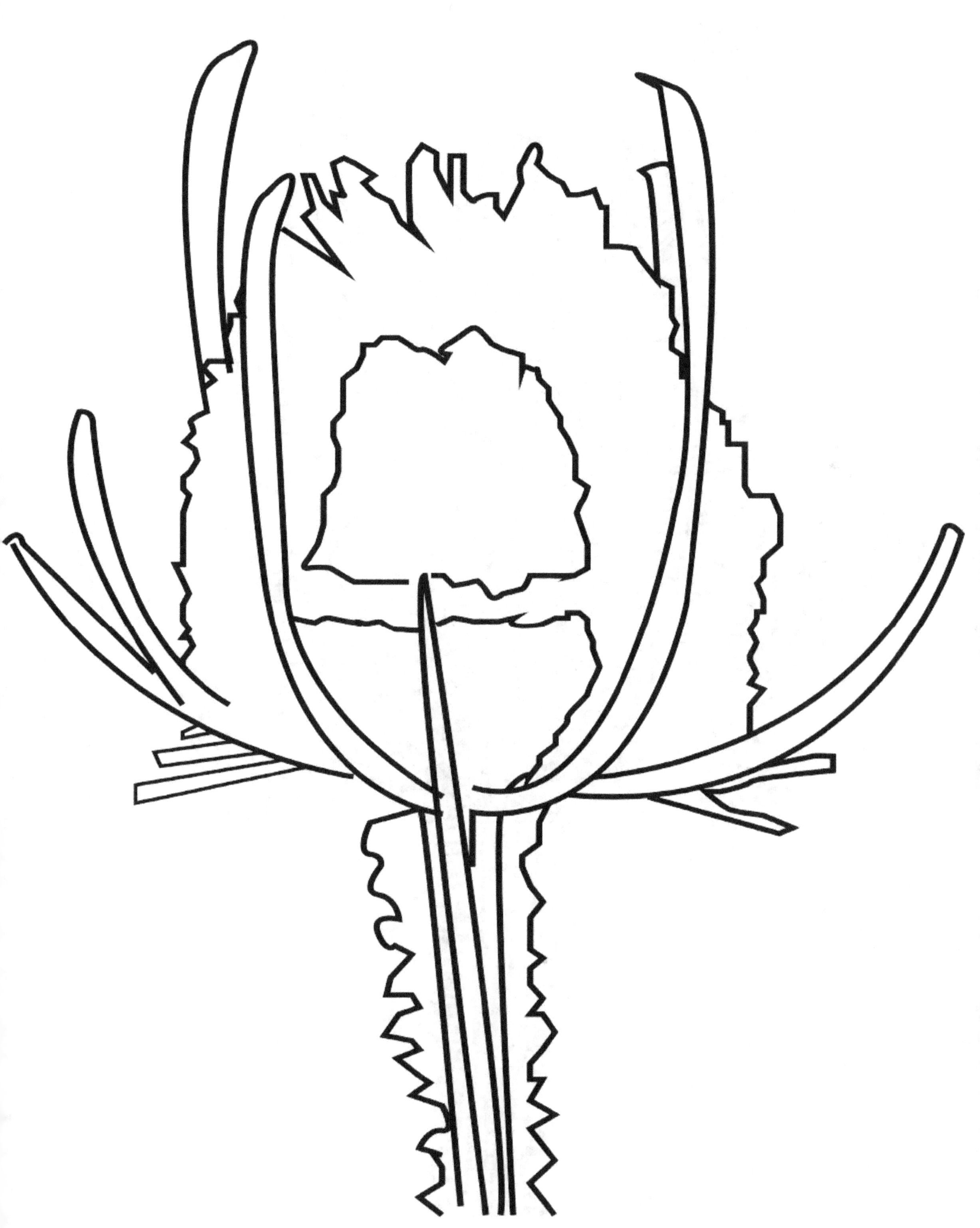

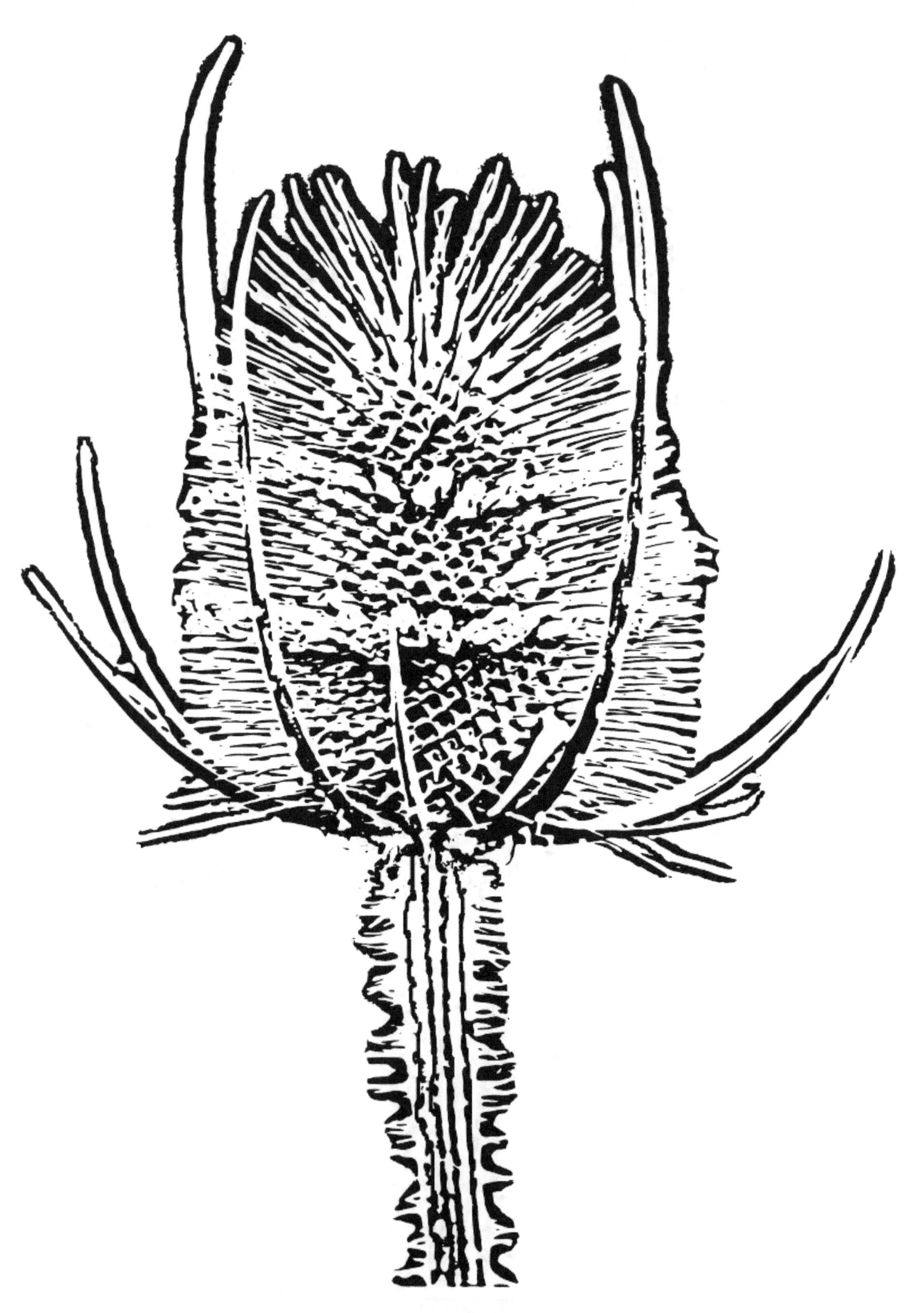

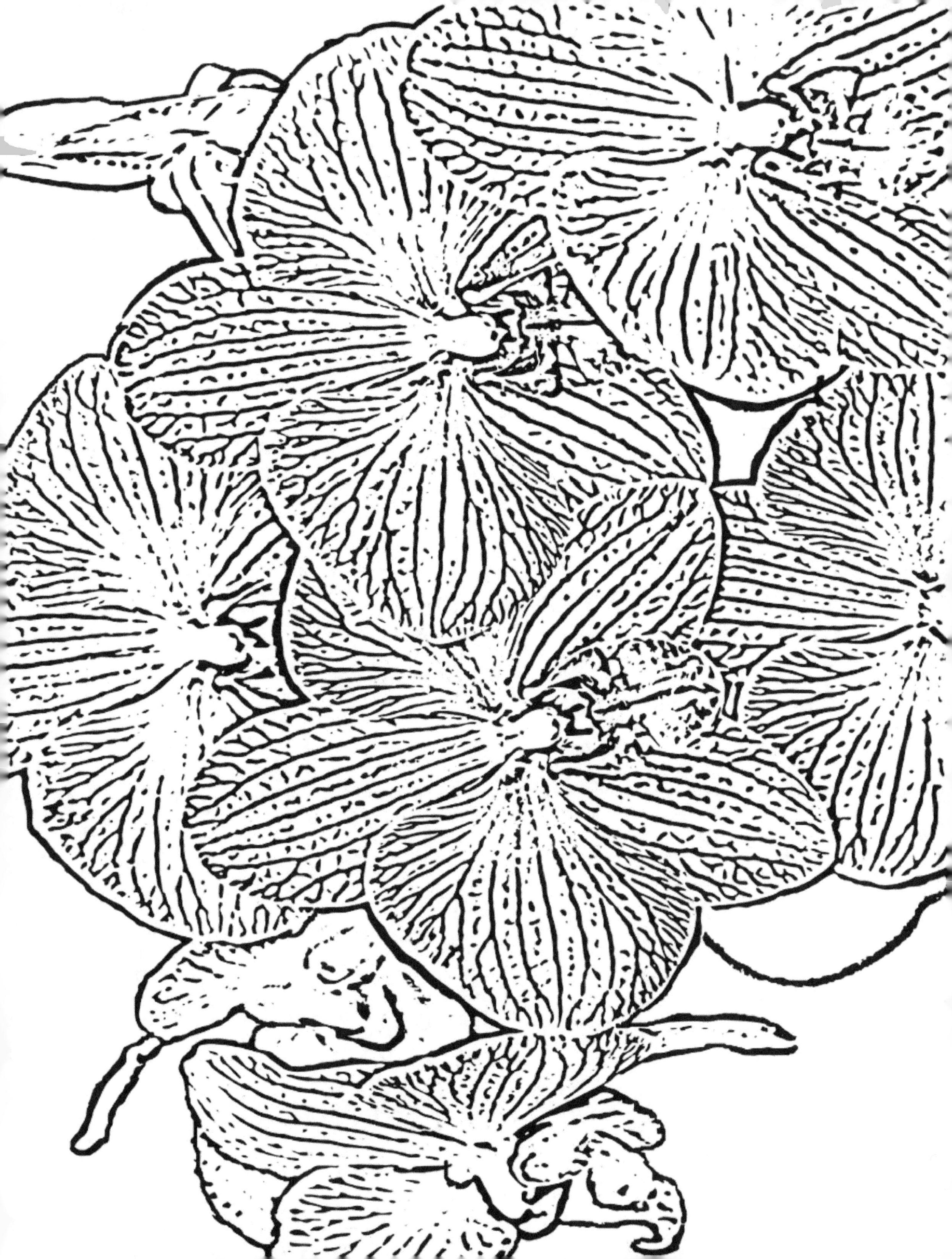